EMMANUEL JOSEPH

Superpower Justice, ICC's Struggle with Major Nations

Copyright © 2025 by Emmanuel Joseph

All rights reserved. No part of this publication may be reproduced, stored or transmitted in any form or by any means, electronic, mechanical, photocopying, recording, scanning, or otherwise without written permission from the publisher. It is illegal to copy this book, post it to a website, or distribute it by any other means without permission.

First edition

*This book was professionally typeset on Reedsy.
Find out more at reedsy.com*

Contents

1. Chapter 1: The Foundation of the International Criminal...   1
2. Chapter 2: The Cold War's Shadow   3
3. Chapter 3: The ICC's First Cases and Growing Pains   5
4. Chapter 4: The United States and the ICC   7
5. Chapter 5: Russia's Role and Reticence   9
6. Chapter 6: China's Calculated Distance   11
7. Chapter 7: The European Union and the ICC   13
8. Chapter 8: African Nations and the ICC: A Complex...   15
9. Chapter 9: The Challenge of Universal Jurisdiction   17
10. Chapter 10: The ICC's Impact on Human Rights   19
11. Chapter 11: Reforming the ICC: Proposals and Prospects   21
12. Chapter 12: The Future of International Justice   23

1

Chapter 1: The Foundation of the International Criminal Court (ICC)

The International Criminal Court (ICC) was established as a beacon of hope for global justice, following the devastation of the two World Wars. In the aftermath of these conflicts, there was a growing consensus among nations that mechanisms were needed to hold individuals accountable for the most heinous crimes. The seeds of the ICC were sown during the Nuremberg and Tokyo trials, which prosecuted war crimes committed during World War II. These trials set important precedents for international law and demonstrated the need for a permanent international court.

The journey to establish the ICC was not straightforward. It involved extensive negotiations and compromises among countries with differing legal traditions and political interests. The Rome Statute, the treaty that established the ICC, was adopted in 1998 after years of deliberation. The statute outlined the court's jurisdiction over genocide, crimes against humanity, war crimes, and later, the crime of aggression. The negotiations highlighted the challenges of achieving global consensus, as some major powers were initially reluctant to support the court.

The ICC officially came into existence on July 1, 2002, when the Rome Statute entered into force. The court's mandate was to prosecute individuals responsible for the most serious crimes of international concern, which are often beyond the capacity of national judicial systems. The ICC's establishment was hailed as a significant step toward ending impunity for perpetrators of mass atrocities. However, from the outset, the court faced numerous challenges, including securing cooperation from member states and ensuring adequate funding and resources.

One of the early challenges for the ICC was defining its jurisdiction and authority. The court's jurisdiction is complementary to national jurisdictions, meaning it can only prosecute cases if national courts are unwilling or unable to do so. This principle of complementarity aimed to respect the sovereignty of states while ensuring accountability for international crimes. However, the ICC's reliance on state cooperation has often led to difficulties in arresting and prosecuting suspects, particularly in cases involving powerful individuals or entities.

As the ICC began its operations, there were high expectations for its role in delivering global justice. The court's initial structure included a presidency, judicial divisions, an office of the prosecutor, and a registry. These bodies were responsible for carrying out the court's functions, from investigating crimes to conducting trials and ensuring the rights of defendants. Despite the optimism surrounding its establishment, the ICC quickly realized that achieving its mandate would require navigating complex political and legal landscapes.

2

Chapter 2: The Cold War's Shadow

The Cold War era cast a long shadow over the development and functioning of international justice systems, including the ICC. The geopolitical tension between the United States and the Soviet Union influenced global politics and international law, shaping the actions and policies of many nations. The ICC, still in its formative years, found itself navigating a complex web of alliances and rivalries. This chapter explores how the Cold War affected the establishment and operation of the ICC, highlighting the court's efforts to maintain impartiality amidst intense political pressure.

During the Cold War, the superpowers' rivalry created an environment of suspicion and mistrust, making it challenging for the ICC to gain widespread support. Both the United States and the Soviet Union were wary of an international court that could potentially prosecute their citizens or allies. This reluctance to fully commit to the ICC stemmed from concerns about sovereignty and the fear that the court could be used as a political tool against them. As a result, the ICC faced significant obstacles in its quest to hold powerful individuals accountable for their actions.

Despite these challenges, the ICC made notable strides in establishing its credibility and independence. The court's early cases, though fraught with difficulties, demonstrated its commitment to impartial justice. These cases often involved lower-ranking officials or individuals from smaller countries, as the court sought to avoid direct confrontations with the superpowers. Nonetheless, the ICC's efforts to prosecute war crimes, genocide, and crimes against humanity during this period laid the groundwork for its future endeavors.

The end of the Cold War brought new opportunities and challenges for the ICC. With the collapse of the Soviet Union and the emergence of new global dynamics, the court faced the task of redefining its role in a rapidly changing world. This chapter delves into the ICC's strategies for adapting to the post-Cold War era, including efforts to expand its jurisdiction and strengthen its mandate. The court's ability to navigate these complexities would prove crucial in its ongoing struggle to deliver justice on a global scale.

Reflecting on the Cold War's impact on the ICC provides valuable insights into the court's evolution and resilience. The lessons learned during this tumultuous period underscore the importance of maintaining impartiality and independence in the face of political pressures. As the ICC continues to grapple with the challenges of prosecuting powerful individuals, the experiences of the Cold War era serve as a testament to the court's enduring commitment to justice.

3

Chapter 3: The ICC's First Cases and Growing Pains

As the ICC began its operations, it faced numerous challenges in prosecuting its first cases. These early trials were crucial in establishing the court's credibility and setting legal precedents. This chapter narrates the ICC's initial cases, highlighting the complexities and controversies that arose. The court's early efforts to address international crimes were met with both praise and criticism, reflecting the high expectations placed upon it.

The first cases prosecuted by the ICC involved individuals accused of committing atrocities during conflicts in various regions. These cases tested the court's ability to navigate complex legal and logistical challenges. One of the landmark cases was that of Thomas Lubanga Dyilo, a Congolese warlord accused of conscripting and using child soldiers. This trial set important legal precedents and demonstrated the ICC's commitment to addressing the recruitment of child soldiers as a serious crime.

However, the ICC's focus on African nations in its early cases led to accusations of bias and selective justice. Critics argued that the court disproportionately targeted African leaders while ignoring crimes committed in other regions. This perception of bias strained the ICC's relationships with some member states and complicated its efforts to secure cooperation for investigations and prosecutions. The court's leadership had to navigate these criticisms while upholding its mandate to deliver justice impartially.

The logistical and bureaucratic hurdles faced by the ICC in its early years were significant. Securing evidence, protecting witnesses, and ensuring fair trials required extensive coordination and resources. The court also had to contend with limited funding and political resistance from various quarters. Despite these challenges, the ICC continued to pursue its mandate, building a body of jurisprudence that would guide its future work.

The ICC's early impact on international justice was a mixed bag of successes and setbacks. While the court succeeded in prosecuting several high-profile cases, it also faced significant obstacles that highlighted the need for reforms and greater international support. This chapter concludes by reflecting on the lessons learned from the ICC's formative years and the implications for its ongoing efforts to hold perpetrators of international crimes accountable.

4

Chapter 4: The United States and the ICC

The relationship between the United States and the ICC has been complex and often contentious. Initially, the US played a significant role in the negotiations leading to the Rome Statute, reflecting its commitment to international justice. However, political and legal concerns led to a shift in US policy, resulting in a fraught relationship with the court. This chapter examines the evolving dynamics between the United States and the ICC, highlighting key events and policies that have shaped their interactions.

The US's initial support for the ICC was rooted in its desire to promote accountability for the most serious international crimes. However, concerns about the court's potential impact on US sovereignty and the prosecution of American personnel led to a re-evaluation of its stance. The American Service-Members' Protection Act (ASPA), enacted in 2002, exemplified the US's apprehensions. The ASPA, also known as the "Hague Invasion Act," authorized the use of military force to free any US or allied personnel detained by the ICC, signaling a significant shift in US policy.

Tensions between the US and the ICC were further exacerbated by the court's investigations into alleged war crimes committed by US forces in Afghanistan. The US government vehemently opposed these investigations, arguing that they infringed on its sovereignty and the jurisdiction of its national courts. This opposition culminated in sanctions against ICC officials, further straining relations between the two entities. The chapter explores these developments and their implications for the ICC's credibility and operations.

Despite these challenges, there have been instances of cooperation and dialogue between the US and the ICC. The US has provided support for ICC investigations and prosecutions in certain cases, particularly those involving atrocities committed by non-state actors. This selective cooperation reflects the complex nature of the US-ICC relationship, characterized by both conflict and collaboration. The chapter examines these instances of cooperation and their impact on the court's work.

The future of the US-ICC relationship remains uncertain, influenced by changing political dynamics and evolving international norms. The chapter concludes by considering the potential for a more constructive engagement between the United States and the ICC. It reflects on the broader implications of this relationship for global perceptions of international justice and the court's ability to fulfill its mandate.

5

Chapter 5: Russia's Role and Reticence

Russia's interactions with the ICC have been marked by skepticism and occasional hostility. As a major global power, Russia's stance towards the ICC has significant implications for the court's effectiveness and legitimacy. This chapter explores Russia's reasons for refusing to ratify the Rome Statute and the challenges this poses for the ICC.

One of the primary reasons for Russia's reticence towards the ICC is its concern about sovereignty and the potential for the court to be used as a tool of political influence. Russia has expressed apprehensions about the ICC's ability to prosecute its nationals and has emphasized the importance of national jurisdiction in handling international crimes. This skepticism was evident in Russia's response to the court's investigations into the conflict in Georgia and allegations of war crimes in Syria.

Specific instances where Russian actions have come under scrutiny by the ICC have further strained relations. The annexation of Crimea and the conflict in Eastern Ukraine are notable examples. The ICC's preliminary examinations and investigations into these situations have led to diplomatic tensions between Russia and the court. Russia's withdrawal of its signature from the Rome Statute in 2016 underscored its opposition to the ICC's involvement in these conflicts.

The broader geopolitical context also plays a crucial role in shaping Russia's stance towards the ICC. Russia's alliances and strategic interests, particularly in the context of its relationships with other major powers and regional actors, influence its approach to international justice. The chapter examines these dynamics and their impact on the ICC's ability to operate effectively in cases involving Russian interests.

Despite the challenges, there have been calls for greater engagement between Russia and the ICC. Some experts argue that constructive dialogue and cooperation could enhance the court's legitimacy and effectiveness. The chapter concludes by reflecting on the prospects for engaging Russia in future ICC initiatives and the potential pathways for improving this complex relationship.

6

Chapter 6: China's Calculated Distance

C hina, one of the world's major powers, has maintained a cautious distance from the ICC. This chapter investigates China's reasons for not joining the ICC, focusing on its concerns about sovereignty and non-interference. China's stance towards the ICC is shaped by its emphasis on national sovereignty and its policy of non-interference in the internal affairs of other countries. This principle is a cornerstone of China's foreign policy and influences its approach to international institutions, including the ICC.

China's concerns about the ICC's potential impact on its sovereignty have led it to refrain from ratifying the Rome Statute. Beijing has expressed reservations about the court's jurisdiction over non-member states and the possibility of politically motivated prosecutions. These concerns were particularly evident during discussions about the ICC's role in addressing international crimes in regions where China has strategic interests, such as Africa and Asia.

Despite its reservations, China has not been entirely disengaged from the ICC. The country has participated in discussions and negotiations related to the court and has expressed support for the principles of international justice. China's growing influence in international institutions and its increasing involvement in global governance have implications for the ICC. This chapter examines China's diplomatic maneuvers and its efforts to balance its national interests with its role in the international community.

The chapter also explores specific cases where China's actions have been relevant to the court's mandate. For example, China's role in the Darfur conflict and its diplomatic efforts to shield Sudanese leaders from ICC prosecution highlight the complexities of its stance. The chapter also explores specific cases where China's actions have been relevant to the court's mandate. For example, China's role in the Darfur conflict and its diplomatic efforts to shield Sudanese leaders from ICC prosecution highlight the complexities of its stance. The chapter delves into the broader implications of China's approach to international justice and the potential impact on the ICC's effectiveness.

China's growing influence in international institutions presents both challenges and opportunities for the ICC. As China continues to expand its global reach, its engagement with international justice mechanisms becomes increasingly significant. The chapter discusses the potential pathways for China to contribute to the ICC's work while addressing its concerns about sovereignty and non-interference. The possibility of China's future involvement in the ICC is a topic of ongoing debate, with implications for the court's legitimacy and authority.

The chapter concludes by assessing the prospects for China's future engagement with international justice mechanisms. It reflects on the potential for dialogue and cooperation between China and the ICC, considering the evolving geopolitical landscape. The chapter underscores the importance of finding common ground to enhance the effectiveness of the ICC and promote global accountability for international crimes.

7

Chapter 7: The European Union and the ICC

The European Union (EU) has been one of the ICC's most steadfast supporters. This chapter explores the nature of the EU's relationship with the court, highlighting key collaborations and contributions. The EU's commitment to international justice is rooted in its foundational principles and its emphasis on human rights and the rule of law. This chapter examines how the EU's support has bolstered the ICC's legitimacy and resources, contributing to its overall mission.

The EU's support for the ICC has been multifaceted, encompassing financial assistance, political backing, and diplomatic engagement. The chapter discusses how the EU has provided substantial funding to support the court's operations, enabling it to carry out investigations and prosecutions. Additionally, the EU has played a crucial role in advocating for universal ratification of the Rome Statute and encouraging member states to cooperate with the ICC.

Despite its strong support, the EU has faced internal challenges and criticisms regarding the court's focus and effectiveness. Some member states have expressed concerns about the ICC's perceived biases and the slow pace of its proceedings. The chapter explores these internal dynamics and the efforts to address them, highlighting the importance of maintaining a united front in support of international justice.

The chapter also examines the EU's broader role in promoting international justice through the ICC. This includes initiatives to strengthen national judicial systems, support victims of international crimes, and enhance cooperation with other international institutions. The EU's commitment to these efforts underscores its dedication to upholding the principles of international justice and accountability.

In conclusion, the chapter reflects on the EU's ongoing support for the ICC and the challenges ahead. It emphasizes the importance of continued collaboration and the need for reforms to enhance the court's effectiveness. The chapter highlights the EU's role in shaping the future of international justice and its potential to contribute to a more accountable and just world.

8

Chapter 8: African Nations and the ICC: A Complex Relationship

The relationship between African nations and the ICC has been one of support mixed with significant contention. Africa's initial enthusiasm for the ICC was rooted in the desire to address impunity for international crimes and promote accountability. However, over time, tensions emerged, leading to a complex and sometimes contentious relationship. This chapter delves into the reasons behind Africa's initial support for the ICC and the subsequent disenchantment.

The chapter begins by exploring the factors that led to Africa's strong support for the ICC during its early years. African nations were instrumental in the drafting and adoption of the Rome Statute, seeing the court as a crucial tool for addressing atrocities committed on the continent. The establishment of the ICC was seen as a positive step towards ending impunity and ensuring justice for victims of serious crimes.

However, the ICC's focus on prosecuting African leaders and officials soon led to allegations of bias and selective justice. Critics argued that the court disproportionately targeted African nations while ignoring crimes committed in other regions. This perception of bias strained the ICC's relationships with African member states and complicated its efforts to secure cooperation for investigations and prosecutions.

The chapter examines specific cases that have contributed to the tensions between African nations and the ICC. High-profile cases, such as the prosecution of Sudanese President Omar al-Bashir and Kenyan President Uhuru Kenyatta, sparked significant controversy and backlash. The African Union's stance towards the ICC, including calls for mass withdrawal from the Rome Statute, further complicated the relationship.

Despite these challenges, there have been efforts to mend the fractured relationship between the ICC and African nations. The chapter discusses initiatives to address the concerns of African member states, including proposals for reform and greater regional involvement in the court's operations. These efforts highlight the potential for renewed collaboration and mutual understanding.

In conclusion, the chapter reflects on the ways forward to mend the relationship between the ICC and African nations. It emphasizes the importance of addressing perceptions of bias and ensuring a more inclusive and effective approach to international justice. The chapter underscores the potential for African nations to play a crucial role in shaping the future of the ICC and promoting global accountability.

9

Chapter 9: The Challenge of Universal Jurisdiction

Universal jurisdiction is a fundamental principle of the ICC, allowing the court to prosecute individuals for serious international crimes regardless of where they were committed. However, the implementation of this principle has been fraught with difficulties. This chapter explores the concept of universal jurisdiction and the practical challenges associated with its enforcement.

The chapter begins by defining universal jurisdiction and its significance in international law. Universal jurisdiction aims to ensure that perpetrators of the most serious crimes, such as genocide, war crimes, and crimes against humanity, do not escape justice due to jurisdictional limitations. The principle is based on the idea that certain crimes are so egregious that they concern the entire international community.

However, the exercise of universal jurisdiction has often led to political and diplomatic conflicts. The chapter discusses cases where attempts to prosecute individuals under universal jurisdiction have been met with resistance from national governments. These cases highlight the tensions between the pursuit of justice and the respect for state sovereignty.

The role of major nations in supporting or undermining universal jurisdiction is a critical aspect of this chapter. The chapter examines how the actions and policies of powerful countries influence the ICC's ability to enforce universal jurisdiction. It also discusses the challenges of securing cooperation from states that are not parties to the Rome Statute.

The chapter also explores the broader implications of universal jurisdiction for international justice. While the principle is essential for holding perpetrators accountable, its implementation requires a delicate balance between legal, political, and diplomatic considerations. The chapter highlights the need for greater international cooperation and coordination to enhance the effectiveness of universal jurisdiction.

In conclusion, the chapter assesses the feasibility of achieving true universal jurisdiction in the current geopolitical climate. It reflects on the challenges and opportunities for the ICC in promoting universal accountability for international crimes. The chapter underscores the importance of continued efforts to strengthen the legal framework and international support for universal jurisdiction.

10

Chapter 10: The ICC's Impact on Human Rights

The ICC's mandate includes the protection and promotion of human rights globally. This chapter evaluates the court's success in this area, highlighting key cases and their outcomes. The chapter begins by discussing the ICC's role in addressing human rights violations and its contributions to the development of international human rights law.

The chapter highlights landmark cases where the ICC has made significant contributions to human rights protection. These cases include prosecutions for crimes such as genocide, crimes against humanity, and war crimes. The chapter discusses the legal precedents set by these cases and their broader impact on international human rights advocacy.

The broader impact of the ICC's work on human rights is also examined. The court's investigations and prosecutions have raised awareness of serious human rights violations and contributed to the global discourse on accountability and justice. The chapter discusses how the ICC's efforts have influenced national and international policies and practices related to human rights protection.

Criticisms of the ICC's approach and effectiveness in promoting human rights are also addressed. The chapter explores concerns about the court's perceived biases, the slow pace of its proceedings, and the challenges of securing cooperation from member states. These criticisms highlight the need for reforms to enhance the ICC's impact on human rights protection.

In conclusion, the chapter reflects on the ways in which the ICC can enhance its impact on human rights protection. It emphasizes the importance of addressing the court's limitations and building on its successes to promote global accountability for human rights violations. The chapter underscores the potential for the ICC to contribute to a more just and equitable world.

11

Chapter 11: Reforming the ICC: Proposals and Prospects

The ICC, like any institution, has room for improvement. This chapter explores various proposals for reforming the court, from procedural changes to structural overhauls. The chapter begins by discussing the challenges and limitations faced by the ICC, including issues related to funding, state cooperation, and the efficiency of its proceedings.

Various proposals for reforming the ICC are examined, including suggestions for streamlining its procedures, enhancing the efficiency of its investigations and trials, and improving its outreach and communication efforts. The chapter discusses the potential benefits and drawbacks of these proposals, considering the perspectives of different stakeholders.

The chapter also explores ongoing efforts to increase the ICC's efficiency and effectiveness. This includes initiatives to strengthen the court's legal framework, enhance its capacity to secure cooperation from member states, and improve its engagement with victims and affected communities. These efforts reflect a commitment to addressing the court's challenges and enhancing its impact on international justice.

The chapter also considers the broader implications of these reforms for the future of the ICC. It discusses the potential for meaningful change and the obstacles that may need to be overcome. The chapter highlights the importance of building consensus among member states and other stakeholders to achieve sustainable and effective reforms.

In conclusion, the chapter reflects on the future of the ICC and the potential for meaningful reform. It emphasizes the importance of continued efforts to enhance the court's efficiency, effectiveness, and legitimacy. The chapter underscores the potential for the ICC to fulfill its mandate and contribute to a more just and accountable world.

12

Chapter 12: The Future of International Justice

The final chapter looks ahead to the future of international justice and the ICC's role within it. It considers the evolving geopolitical landscape and the challenges and opportunities it presents for the ICC. As the world becomes increasingly interconnected, the ICC faces the task of adapting to new realities while staying true to its mandate of delivering justice for the most serious international crimes.

The chapter begins by examining the evolving geopolitical landscape and its implications for the ICC. Emerging global powers, shifting alliances, and new forms of conflict present both challenges and opportunities for the court. The chapter discusses how the ICC can navigate these complexities while maintaining its independence and impartiality. It also explores the potential impact of technological advancements, such as cyber warfare and artificial intelligence, on the court's work.

The chapter then delves into potential new areas of focus for the ICC, such as environmental crimes and crimes related to the exploitation of natural resources. These emerging issues highlight the need for the ICC to expand its mandate and address a broader range of international crimes. The chapter explores the legal and practical challenges associated with prosecuting these new types of crimes and the potential benefits for global justice.

The chapter also reflects on the broader implications of the ICC's work for global justice and accountability. The court's efforts to hold perpetrators accountable for serious international crimes have had a significant impact on the international legal landscape. The chapter discusses the importance of continued support for the ICC from the international community and the need for reforms to enhance its effectiveness.

In conclusion, the chapter offers an optimistic vision of a world where international justice is truly universal and effective. It emphasizes the importance of international cooperation, strong legal frameworks, and a commitment to upholding human rights and the rule of law. The chapter underscores the potential for the ICC to contribute to a more just and accountable world, where perpetrators of serious international crimes are held accountable and justice is served.

The Book Description

Superpower Justice: ICC's Struggle with Major Nations

In the wake of global conflicts and the pursuit of justice, the International Criminal Court (ICC) was founded to hold individuals accountable for the most serious crimes known to humanity. But the journey of the ICC has been anything but straightforward. This book delves deep into the intricate and often contentious relationship between the ICC and major world powers.

Superpower Justice: ICC's Struggle with Major Nations explores the foundation of the ICC, tracing its origins from the Nuremberg and Tokyo trials, through to the adoption of the Rome Statute and the court's establishment. It examines the impact of the Cold War on the ICC's early years, the court's first landmark cases, and the logistical challenges that defined its formative period.

The narrative provides an insightful analysis of the complex dynamics between the ICC and powerful nations like the United States, Russia, and China. It scrutinizes their reluctance to fully embrace the court's mandate and the political maneuvers employed to shield their actions from international scrutiny. The book also sheds light on the unwavering support from the European Union and the turbulent relationship with African nations, addressing allegations of bias and selective justice.

CHAPTER 12: THE FUTURE OF INTERNATIONAL JUSTICE

Through detailed chapters, the book evaluates the principle of universal jurisdiction, the ICC's contributions to human rights, and the ongoing efforts to reform the court for greater efficiency and effectiveness. Finally, it looks ahead to the future of international justice, exploring new areas of focus and the evolving geopolitical landscape.

Superpower Justice is an essential read for anyone interested in understanding the challenges and triumphs of the ICC as it strives to deliver justice in a world where power dynamics and international law often collide. It paints a comprehensive picture of the ICC's struggle to uphold its mandate against the backdrop of global politics and the pursuit of accountability.

www.ingramcontent.com/pod-product-compliance
Lightning Source LLC
LaVergne TN
LVHW020744090526
838202LV00057BA/6218